CONTENTS

Introduction

President Obama's trade policy seeks to promote growth, support more well-paying jobs in the United States, and strengthen the middle class. Trade policy done right – through proactive enforcement of existing agreements and the negotiation of new, high standard agreements – is among the nation's best tools to address the challenges of globalization and technological change and promote American interests and values.

Trade has played an indispensable role in America's recovery from the Great Recession. Since the end of the recession in mid-2009, the increase in U.S. exports has contributed nearly one-third of our overall economic growth. Last year, U.S. exports reached **$2.35 trillion**, a record-breaking amount that supported over **11 million** good-paying American jobs. With those jobs paying up to **18 percent more** than jobs not related to exports, trade policy has an important role to play in raising wages and living standards for the middle class. Partially as a result of our exporting success, our economy continues to grow: Job creation is happening at the fastest rate since the 1990s, and the budget deficit is falling at the fastest rate since the 1940s. After nearly two decades in decline, factories are opening in this country again and manufacturing jobs are starting to return from overseas.

President Obama's trade policy seeks to promote growth, support more well-paying jobs in the United States, and strengthen the middle class.

IN 2014,
THE UNITED STATES EXPORTED
MORE MADE-IN-AMERICA
GOODS AND SERVICES THAN
EVER BEFORE: $2.35 TRILLION.
U.S. EXPORTS SUPPORTED
11.7 MILLION AMERICAN JOBS.

Today, "**Made in America**" is making a comeback:

- More American small businesses are exporting than ever before.

- American farmers are exporting more than ever before.

- American manufacturers and service providers are exporting more than ever before, with manufacturing growing faster than the rest of the economy.

Behind these statistics are flesh-and-blood success stories for working families: the auto parts firm that would have closed its line and gone dark had it not been for overseas markets; the craftsman now finding customers around the world via the internet; and the technology company or the family farm that secured that new contract abroad. There are hundreds of thousands more stories like it.

Yet despite the proven benefits of trade, there continues to be uneasiness around pursuing new trade opportunities. That is understandable. Changes in technology and automation, combined with the continued pace of globalization, have increased pressure on wages and contributed to the sense that there are fewer opportunities for working Americans.

The concern is legitimate.

The question is what are we going to do about it?

Trade policy done right is how we protect American workers and jobs, create a more fair and level playing field, and ensure that it is the United States that leads in defining the rules of the road. But the reality is that Americans are already competing against the rest of the world.

We already have one of the most open markets on the planet. Our tariffs on imports are extremely low – less than 1.5 percent on average – and we do not use non-tariff barriers to prevent other countries from selling their goods and services in the United States.

Whether we continue to pursue trade agreements or not, the United States will continue to see foreign imports because consumers demand them and we have virtually no barriers to imports.

The same is not true for other countries, many of which have high tariffs and non-tariff barriers to discriminate against American products; provide unfair subsidies; and encourage development without concern for the environment or the rights of workers. All of these barriers separate American producers from the 95 percent of global consumers who live outside our borders. That is why American trade agreements benefit American workers.

We already have one of the most open markets on the planet.

The same is not true for other countries.

That is why American trade agreements benefit American workers.

UNLOCKING OPPORTUNITY THROUGH TRADE

EXPORTS SUPPORT GOOD-PAYING AMERICAN JOBS

EVERY $1 BILLION IN EXPORTS = SUPPORTS 5,200 - 7,000 JOBS

MAIN STREET JOBS	BETTER PAYING JOBS	GROWING EXPORTS
98% OF ALL U.S. EXPORTERS ARE SMALL BUSINESSES	EXPORT JOBS PAY ON AVG UP TO 18% MORE THAN NON-EXPORT JOBS	U.S EXPORTS HAVE INCREASED NEARLY 50% SINCE 2009
98%	Up to 18%	50%

USTR.GOV

Record U.S. Exports Have Made a Major Contribution to Our Economic Recovery…

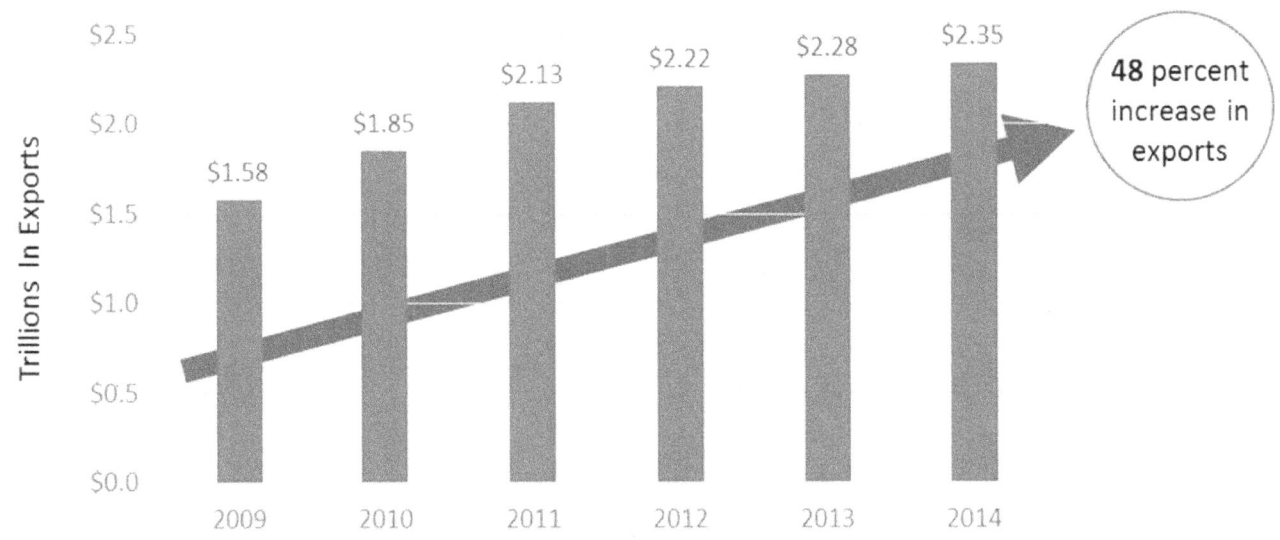

… Including Supporting Additional High Wage Jobs

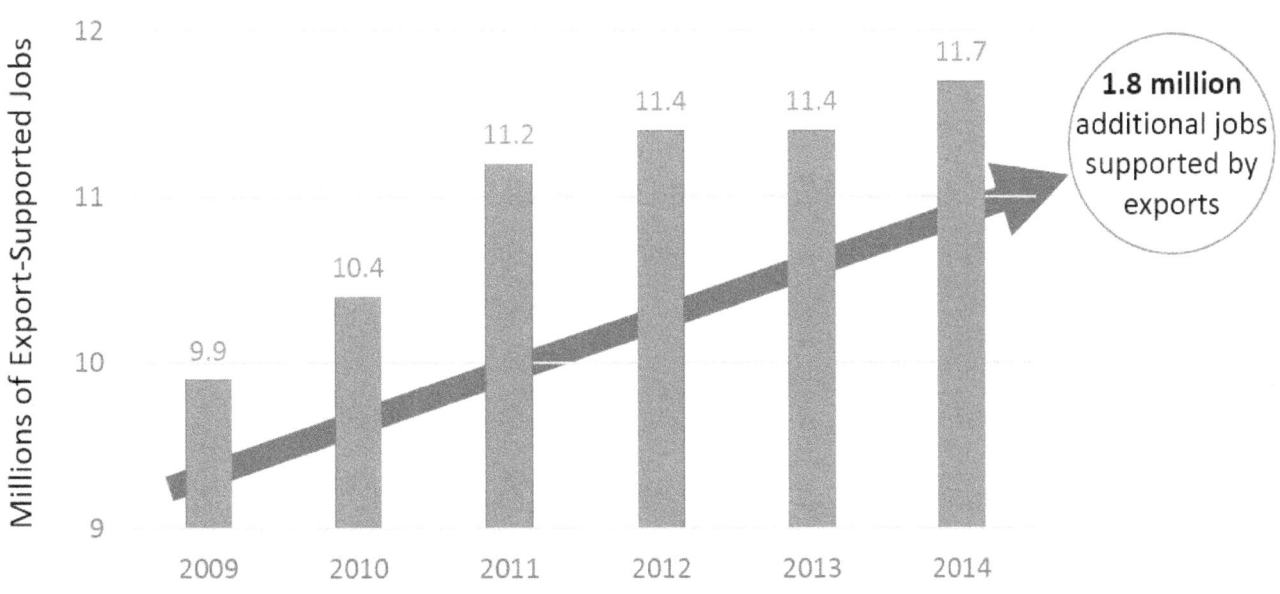

Market Opportunities Overwhelmingly Beyond Our Borders

95% of the world's consumers are outside our borders

80% of the world's purchasing power is outside our borders

Asia's Middle Class is the Fastest Growing Market in the World...

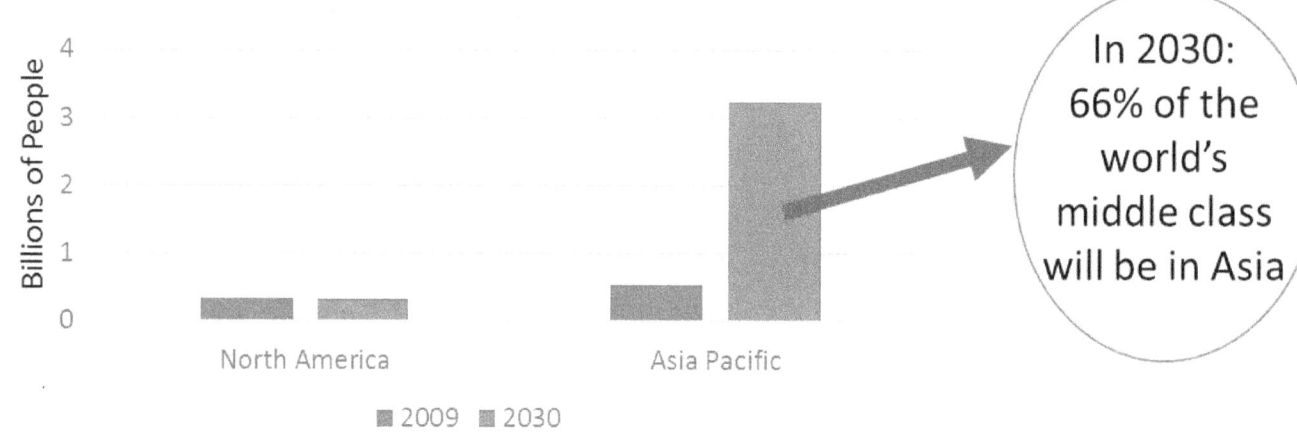

In 2030: 66% of the world's middle class will be in Asia

...And Will Drive Global Middle Class Demand in the Coming Decades

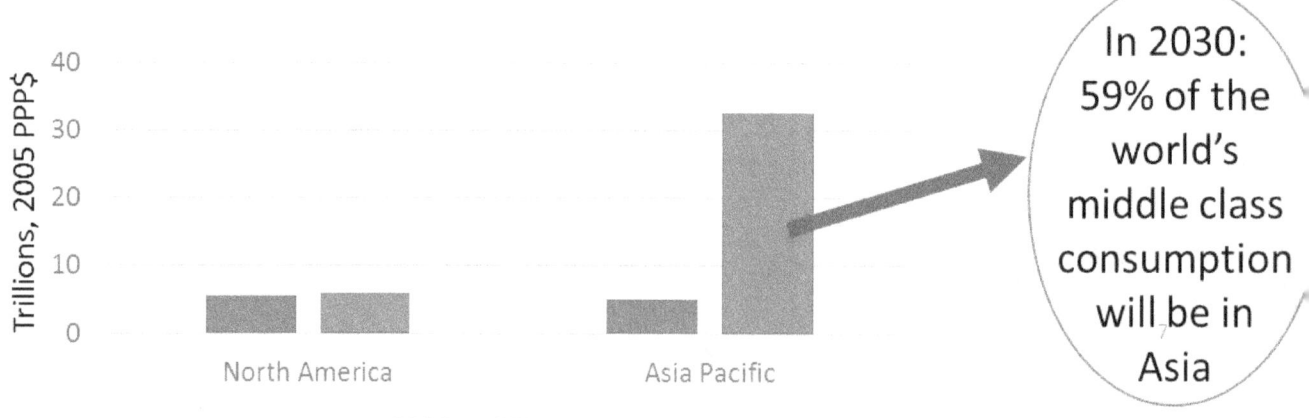

In 2030: 59% of the world's middle class consumption will be in Asia

Taking on the Status Quo

If the playing field is level and the competition is fair, American workers and businesses can and will win.

The pace of globalization and technological change is not slowing down. We need to take on that challenge. Consider this: in the last five years, the capacity of the world's container fleets has grown by 50 percent. The number of internet users has doubled and the amount of internet traffic has tripled. The world's urban population has grown by hundreds of millions of people.

These trends are not going away.

Expansion in Global Commerce and Communication: Just Over the Last Five Years

The world's container-fleet capacity has expanded from 10.8 million TEUs to 16.1 million TEUs

World Internet traffic has grown from 8 petabytes to 40 petabytes of data per month

The global Internet user community from 2 billion to 3 billion people

The worldwide urban population has grown from 3.5 billion to 3.8 billion people – up from 3 billion ten years ago

The question we face is not whether we can roll back the tide of globalization. It is whether we are going to shape it or be shaped by it, whether we are going to do everything we can to ensure that it reflects our interest and our values – or to let other countries define it for us.

Americans do not passively stand by. We engage. We shape. We lead.

History tells us that there is an American tradition. Americans don't passively stand by. We engage. We shape. We lead. That is precisely what we are doing right now in trade.

By leading on trade, the United States can level the playing field for our workers and businesses. We can knock down barriers to U.S. exports and raise standards around the world. Both our interests and our values are at stake when it comes to protecting worker rights and the environment, promoting innovation and access to that innovation, and maintaining a free and open Internet.

That's why we've insisted on putting the highest labor and environmental standards of any trade agreement in the Trans-Pacific Partnership (TPP), which we're negotiating with 11 countries in the Asia Pacific. When completed, this agreement will boost middle class paychecks here at home as well as working conditions and environmental protections in the world's fastest-growing region. In the Asia Pacific and elsewhere, we can give more Americans a fair shot in global markets by forging trade agreements that are progressive and pro-growth.

Taken together, these efforts constitute the most ambitious trade agenda in history – economically and strategically. The United States already has a number of strengths that make it an attractive place to invest and do business, including a talented and productive workforce, strong rule of law, and increasingly abundant sources of affordable energy. Through our trade agenda, we are seeking to put the United States at the center of a trade zone covering nearly two-thirds of the global economy. That will help make America the world's production platform of choice, increasing U.S. exports and attracting more employers that want to invest in the United States, hire American workers, and sell American goods and services to the world.

Trade policy is a lever for encouraging investment in the United States, creating more high-paying jobs, and combatting wage stagnation and income inequality.

In this sense, our trade policy is a lever for encouraging investment in the United States, creating more high-paying jobs and combatting wage stagnation and income inequality.

America's Role in the World

By strengthening the U.S. economy – America's foundation of power – our trade policy helps to protect the strategic capabilities our economy supports. Increasingly, however, the economic clout that trade creates is itself an important source of influence in world affairs. Exercising that influence, this agenda advances three strategic objectives: strengthening our partners and allies, establishing and enforcing rules of the road, and spurring broad-based, inclusive development.

Trade agreements can build mutual strength with our partners and signal the importance of these partnerships to the world. For example, through the Transatlantic Trade and Investment Partnership (T-TIP), we are deepening our economic relationship with the European Union (EU), which is already the world's largest and covers $1 trillion in annual trade, $4 trillion in investment, and supports 13 million jobs on both sides of the Atlantic. At a time of geopolitical uncertainty on the periphery of Europe, the T-TIP reminds the world that our transatlantic partnership is second-to-none.

Our agreements also bring stability to critical regions in flux. A main pillar of our rebalance toward Asia, the TPP will set rules of the road for nearly 40 percent of the global economy, including the world's fastest growing region. It will strengthen habits of cooperation among our partners. And it underscores that the United States is – and always will be – a Pacific power, and that our future is very much intertwined with the stability and prosperity of the Asia-Pacific region.

Our trade policy aims not only to update the global economic architecture but also to expand it through efforts like the African Growth and Opportunity Act. The cornerstone of U.S. trade policy with sub-Saharan Africa since 2000, this program has supported job growth in Africa and the United States and created countless market opportunities for American businesses. Updating and renewing our relationships to reflect changes within Africa and between African countries and their trading partners would send a strong message that America remains deeply committed to this dynamic region and to promoting broad-based development through trade.

Strategic objectives strongly reinforce the economic merits of trade. For example, working with developing nations to alleviate poverty and foster economic growth simultaneously creates better market opportunities for U.S. exporters. By leading on environmental, labor, and other issues, we can launch a race to the top, rather than be subject to a race to the bottom. At a time when our open, rules-based system is competing against alternative models, advancing these objectives will help revitalize the global trading system, allowing the United States to continue to play a leading role and ensuring that system reflects American interests and values.

Our efforts in 2015 will build on successful 2014 initiatives. Last year, the United States made substantial progress toward concluding the TPP. With the European Union, we made a fresh start in negotiations for the T-TIP. We played a critical role in realizing the first fully multilateral trade agreement in the history of the World Trade Organization (WTO), the Trade Facilitation Agreement (TFA), and made significant progress in negotiations to expand the scope of goods covered by the WTO Information Technology Agreement (ITA). Additionally, along with 13 other partners, we launched negotiations on the Environmental Goods Agreement (EGA) in Geneva.

This will be a historic year for U.S. trade policy. In 2015, we will conclude negotiations with TPP countries. We will make significant progress with the EU toward a T-TIP agreement to further strengthen the world's largest trade relationship. We will advance negotiations on the Trade in Services Agreement (TiSA). We will work with Congress to update and renew the African Growth and Opportunities Act (AGOA) for the longest term possible. We will continue fighting for America's trade rights, strengthening the multilateral trading system at the WTO, expanding the ITA, and continuing negotiations on an EGA. These are just some of the many areas where American leadership on trade will increase U.S. exports to the world while supporting job growth here at home.

To further strengthen America's ability to lead on trade, President Obama has called on Congress to work with him to secure approval of bipartisan Trade Promotion Authority (TPA). TPA is a critical tool for Congress to update and assert its role in trade policy and to guide current and future negotiations.

For more than 80 years, since the time of FDR, Democrats and Republicans have worked together on similar measures to promote American exports and create jobs. This year, we have an opportunity to build on that tradition by modernizing TPA to address new issues and to update Congress's role in trade policy.

Spotlight: Trade Promotion Authority

Trade Promotion Authority is the product of decades of evolution during which time Congress has strengthened its role in overseeing trade policy. The first trade authority dates back to 1934, when the New Deal Congress allowed President Franklin D. Roosevelt to negotiate tariff reductions. Every American president has had trade negotiating authority since then, except Richard Nixon. The original trade negotiating authority allowed the President to enter into trade agreements without requiring subsequent Congressional approval. That was a delegation – and that's not the way it's done anymore.

The first trade authority dates back to 1934, when the New Deal Congress allowed FDR to negotiate tariff reductions. Trade authority has been revised and reauthorized by Congress on 18 different occasions.

In 1974, Congress passed new trade authority, establishing strong requirements for collaboration between Congress and the Executive Branch, imposing specific negotiating objectives and extensive new consultation requirements on the Executive Branch, while fully retaining Congress's Constitutional prerogative to make all final determinations about whether trade agreements entered into law. Trade authority has been subsequently revised and reauthorized by Congress on 18 different occasions, by Congresses of both parties.

President	Legislative Action	Year	Control
Roosevelt (D)	Reciprocal Trade Agreements Act	1934	Democrat
	Renewal	1937	Democrat
	Renewal	1940	Democrat
	Renewal	1943	Democrat
	Renewal	1945	Democrat
Truman (D)	Trade Agreements Extension Act	1948	Republican
	Renewal	1949	Democrat
	Renewal	1951	Democrat
Eisenhower (R)	Trade Agreements Extension Act	1953	Republican
	Renewal	1954	Republican
	Renewal	1955	Democrat
	Renewal	1958	Democrat
Kennedy (D)	Trade Expansion Act	1962	Democrat
Johnson (D)	Trade Expansion Act	1962	Democrat
Ford (R)	Trade Act	1974	Democrat
Carter (D)	Trade Act	1974	Democrat
	Trade Agreements Act	1979	Democrat
Reagan (R)	Trade Agreements Act	1979	Democrat
	Trade and Tariffs Act	1985	R Senate / D House
	Omnibus Trade Act	1988	Democrat
Bush I (R)	Omnibus Trade Act	1988	Democrat
Clinton (D)	Renewal	1993	Democrat
Bush II (R)	Trade Act	2002	D Senate / R House

Under TPA, Congress cedes no authority to the President.

Under TPA, Congress cedes no authority to the President. Presidents are always able to negotiate with foreign countries – but only Congress can implement a trade agreement. Congress retains all of its Constitutional authority and, as provided for in the Constitution, either chamber of Congress can change its procedures at any time – including revoking TPA. This is exactly what House Democrats did in 2008 when they were unhappy with the outcome of trade negotiations.

TPA was last updated in 2002. A lot has happened since then. As the economy changes, our approach to trade should change, too. New TPA legislation should address the digital economy, state-owned enterprises, and, for the first time ever, require by law that all future trade agreements include fully enforceable labor and environmental provisions. TPA should be updated to reflect today's economy. Through TPA, Congress sets very clear priorities and objectives for the Executive branch, while establishing a set of notification and consultation procedures that allows the U.S. to speak with one voice in negotiations.

TPA should be updated to reflect Congressional priorities for today's economy.

Some call TPA "fast track" – but there is nothing fast about it.

Some call TPA "fast track" – but there is nothing fast about it. Most agreements take years to negotiate during which time they undergo congressional scrutiny. First, Congress receives a 90 day notification before negotiations begin with trading partners. After years of negotiation, when negotiations are completed, Congress is provided another 90 day notification. Months later, when implementing legislation is introduced, Congress takes up to 90 legislative days (typically several months) to hold hearings, convene sessions for drafting implementing legislation, and ultimately vote on agreements. Before implementing legislation heads to the floor Congressional Committees issue detailed reports, including on whether negotiating objectives have been met or not.

As Franklin Roosevelt said 80 years ago when he first asked for trade negotiating authority: "The world does not stand still." In recent years, Asia-Pacific countries have entered over 200 agreements, moving trade opportunities away from the United States and putting U.S. companies and workers at a disadvantage. China has been the largest beneficiary. That is a status quo that is not acceptable. To keep strengthening our economy, we need better trade rules that protect American jobs and workers and that help us export our goods around the world.

It's time to give the President the tools he has asked for – to bring home the most progressive trade agreements in history for U.S. workers. Approving an updated TPA is the first step in that process.

We're Not Out There Alone

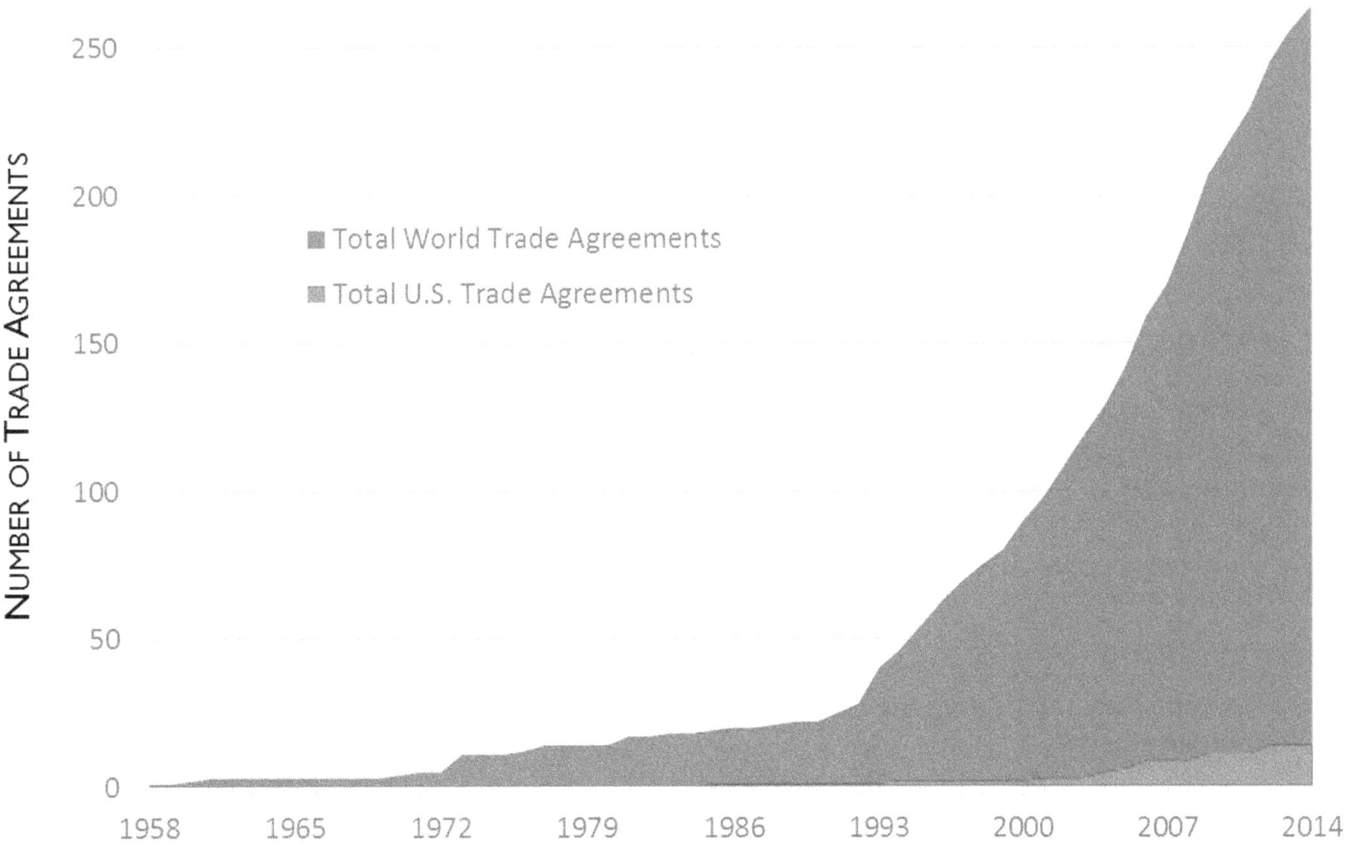

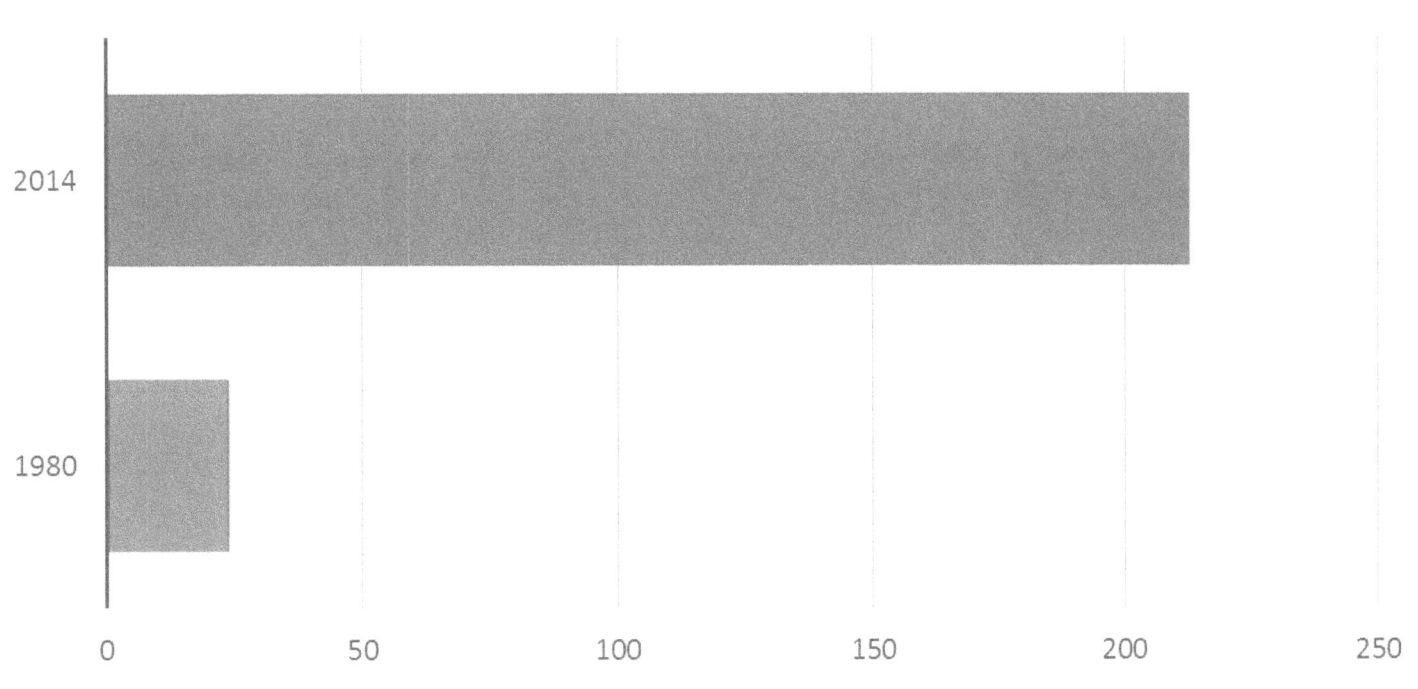

Number of Trade Agreements

- Total World Trade Agreements
- Total U.S. Trade Agreements

250
200
150
100
50
0

1958 1965 1972 1979 1986 1993 2000 2007 2014

Growth in Trade Agreements in the Asia-Pacific

2014

1980

0   50   100   150   200   250

The Path Not Taken

What price would we pay in terms of U.S. interests and values if we were to abandon the ambitious trade agenda proposed by the President?

First, we would lose the opportunities to create new, high-paying jobs through expanded exports that are so important to our economic recovery. Other countries would get preferential access to some of the largest and fastest-growing markets in the world at our expense. Our firms would find themselves at a disadvantage, creating incentives for them to either drop out of the competition or move their production overseas to access those markets.

Second, we would lose the opportunity to secure enforceable commitments on labor and environmental standards – missing a valuable chance to promote core labor standards and acceptable conditions of work; and diminishing our ability to protect the marine environment, curb illegal and over-fishing, combat wildlife trafficking and illegal logging, and protect sensitive areas. Rather, we would cede the rule-setting to others for whom protecting workers and the environment are not priorities.

Third, we would limit both our ability to protect American invention, artistic creativity, and research, and our ability to develop creative ways to speed the flow of new medicines to patients and further the freedom of people to search, buy and create on the Internet. Rather, we would see an accelerated rise of "data nationalism" and a digital world that begins to erect barriers rather than transcend them.

Right now, there are 525 million middle class consumers in Asia alone. By 2030, there are expected to be 3.2 billion middle class consumers in Asia, more than 8 times the size of what the U.S. market is expected to be at that time. Those consumers will want better diets and more protein. They will want entertainment, games and software. They will want to engage in e-commerce and order products from all over the world. They will want to save and invest for their families' future. They will want to breathe clean air, drink clean water and support a sustainable environment. They will want clean energy products and equipment to build roads and schools. They will want cars and trucks and airplanes.

Who will provide these goods and services? Will it be American workers, farmers and ranchers, or their competitors from other countries? Will we have access to markets and terms on which we can compete, or will we be left on the sidelines?

Other countries are not standing by and waiting for us to act. They are busy negotiating their own deals, trying to gain preferential market access to countries, setting rules of the road that do not reflect our values. And they do not put the emphasis we do on raising labor and environmental standards, protecting intellectual property rights, promoting access to innovation, preserving the freedom of the Internet or putting disciplines on state-owned enterprises.

We face a choice: Work to raise the bar or stay on the sidelines as other countries write the rules of the game. Promote a race to the top or acquiesce to a race to the bottom which we cannot win and which our values tell us we should not run. That is not in the interest of America's workers and America's families.

Job Creation and Economic Growth

In 2015, the Administration will actively pursue a range of initiatives to expand globally competitive U.S. exports in our manufacturing and agriculture sectors. A revitalized U.S. manufacturing sector continues to play a key role in the future of our economy. As American manufacturers grow our capacity to produce more advanced and value-added goods, consumers around the world continue to place a high value on products made in America.

In 2014, the United States exported $1.4 trillion of manufactured goods, which accounted for 86 percent of all U.S. goods exports and 60 percent of U.S. total exports.

This strong performance supports good-paying U.S. jobs, contributing to the nearly 900,000 manufacturing jobs that the economy has added since 2010.

To further support the growth of advanced manufacturing and associated high-quality jobs here at home, in 2015 the Obama Administration will continue to pursue trade policies aimed at keeping American manufacturers competitive with their global peers.

Throughout our trade negotiations, we aim to discipline the use of trade and regulatory measures that create barriers to U.S. exports, level the playing field between SOEs and private firms, ensure that rules of origin promote manufacturing in the United States, and increase the efficiency of the global supply chain and thereby create incentives for manufacturers to locate in the United States.

As the U.S. knowledge and innovation economy continues to grow in the 21st century, we have become the world's largest trader in services. For the United States, services account for over three-quarters of U.S. private sector GDP and four out of five jobs. Thanks to a vibrant and open domestic market, the United States is highly competitive in services trade, routinely recording an annual surplus on the order of $200 billion. With every $1 billion in services exports supporting an estimated 7,000 U.S. jobs, expanding services trade globally will unlock new opportunities for Americans.

How Are Export-Intensive Industries Different?
Higher Wages, Higher Productivity, Higher Value-Added

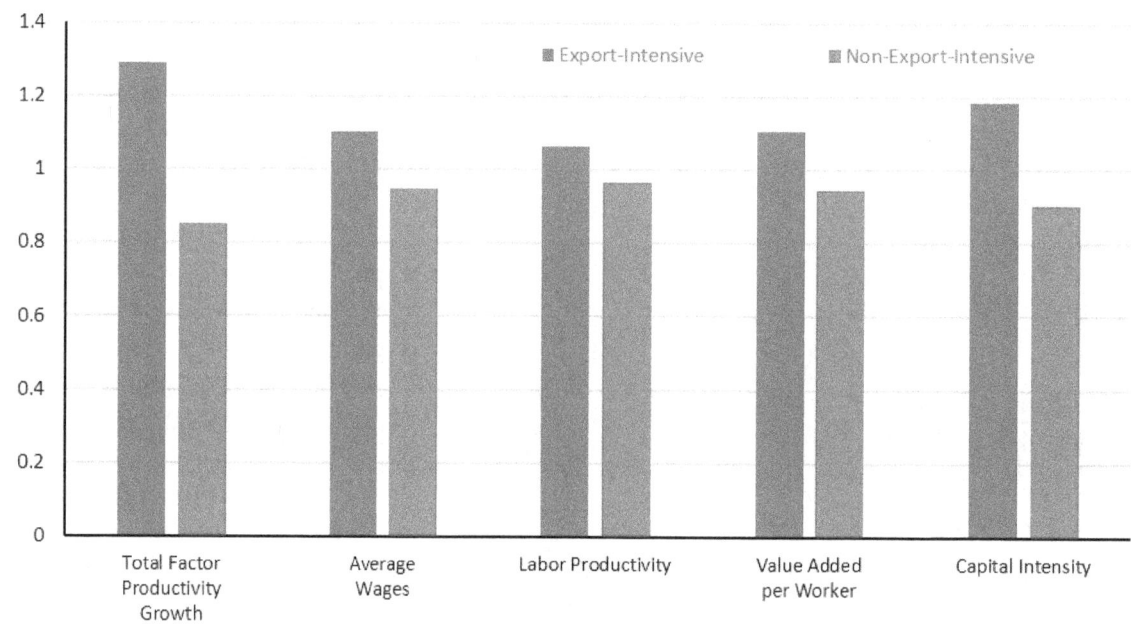

Since the beginning of the Obama Administration, the agricultural sector has been a bright spot for exports, estimated to support more than one million American jobs throughout the U.S. agricultural supply chain. In 2014, the United States exported another record amount of $155.1 billion of food and agricultural goods to consumers around the world.

In 2015, the Administration will continue to focus on combatting the growing number of unwarranted Sanitary and Phytosanitary (SPS) barriers to trade by advocating for science-based standards in support of additional exports of U.S. food and agricultural products. To realize the full benefits of our existing trade agreements, we will continue to use the consultative mechanisms established in each agreement to ensure that all relevant commitments are upheld. Our efforts in agriculture also will include an ongoing push in plurilateral discussions on aligning regulatory approaches affecting trade in products derived from modern biotechnology by building alliances with like-minded countries and utilizing international standards organizations both to grow U.S. agricultural exports and to improve global food security.

Spotlight: Manufacturing

After more than a decade of job losses, we've **added nearly 900,000 manufacturing jobs** over five straight years of job growth. U.S. **manufacturing is now growing at nearly twice the rate of the economy**, the longest sustained period of outpacing the economy since the 1960s. Manufacturing output has increase 30 percent since the end of the recession, contributing to growing manufacturing exports.

Manufacturing Exports Continue to Grow

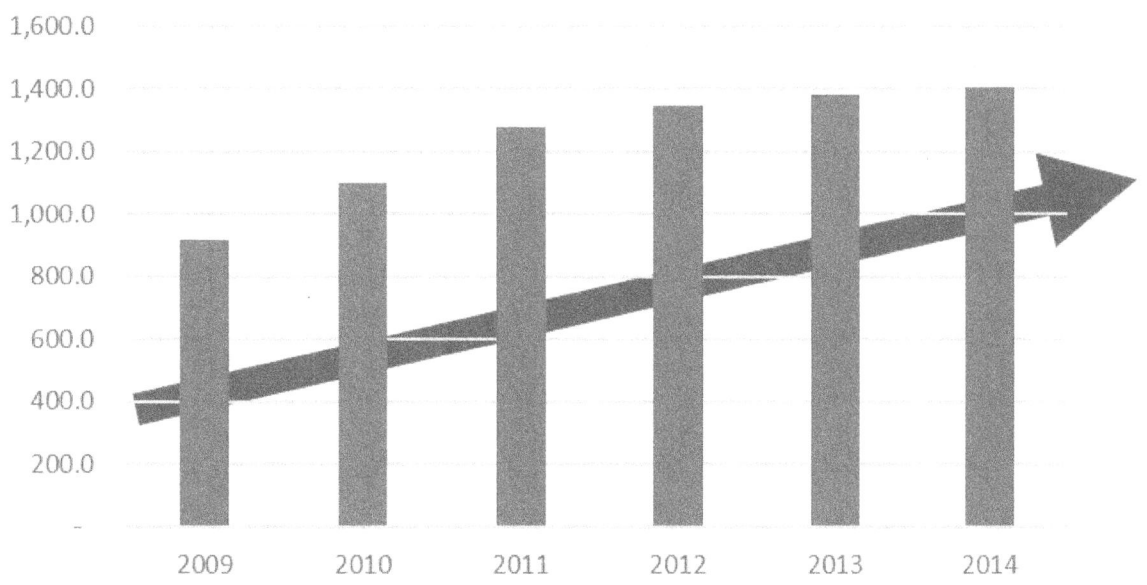

U.S. manufacturing plays an outsized role in supporting and driving American innovation, and increasingly our ability to manufacture undergirds our future ability to innovate.

If the U.S. manufacturing sector were a country, it would be the 9th largest economy in the world. 1 out of every 7 American private sector workers works in a job supported by manufacturing.

At the same time, U.S. companies are looking to move production back to the United States from China. 54 percent of companies surveyed in 2013 were actively considering moving manufacturing back from China to the U.S. – nearly a 50 percent increase over 2012.

Nearly 900,000 new manufacturing jobs

Record manufacturing exports

Manufacturing growing at twice the rate of the economy – fastest growth since the 1960s

U.S. ranked the best place to invest for the first time since 2001

AMERICAN MANUFACTURING IS GROWING STRONGER EVERY DAY

SINCE FEBRUARY 2010, AMERICAN MANUFACTURING HAS ADDED NEARLY 900,000 JOBS, THE FASTEST PACE OF JOB GROWTH SINCE THE 1990S.

THEN: 2000 - 2010   NOW: 2010 - 2014

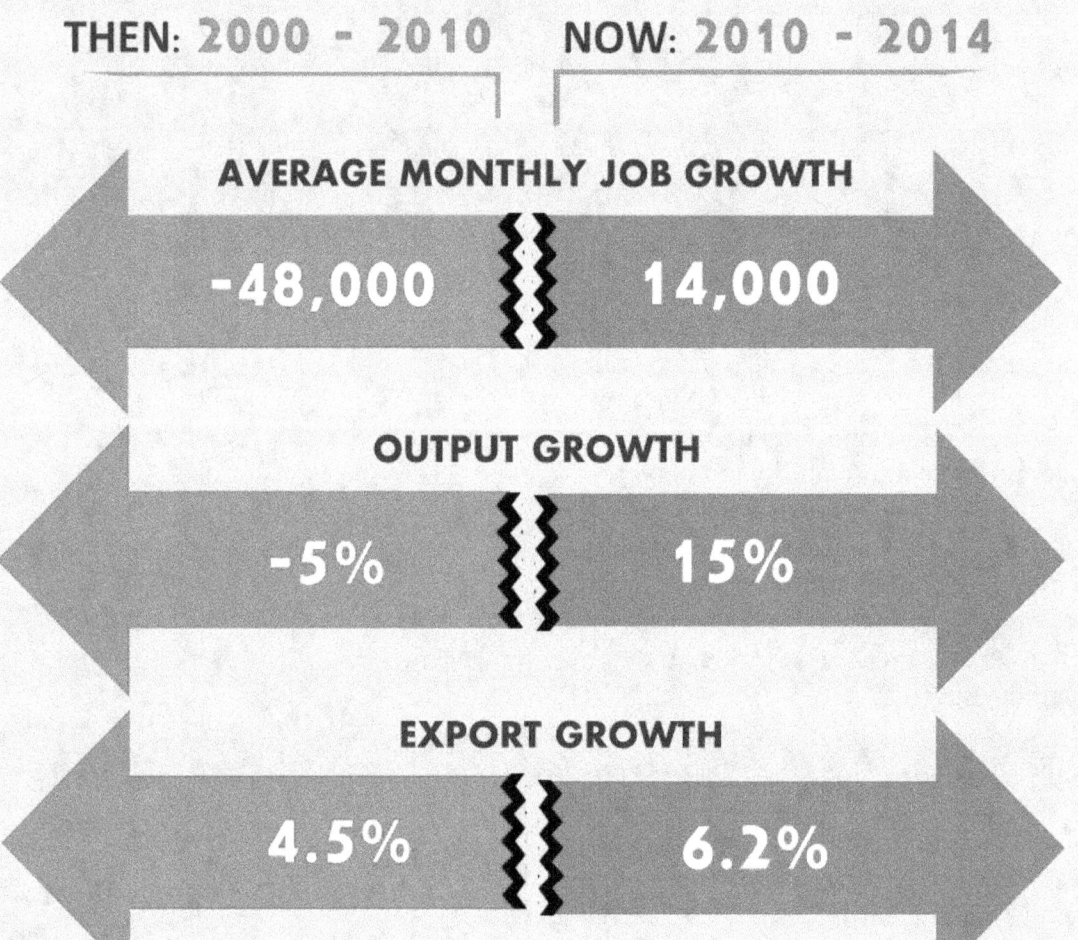

AVERAGE MONTHLY JOB GROWTH

-48,000   14,000

OUTPUT GROWTH

-5%   15%

EXPORT GROWTH

4.5%   6.2%

Spotlight: Agriculture

In 2014, exports of U.S. food and agricultural products reached a **record $155.1 billion** – the culmination of the **strongest six year period of agricultural exports in our nation's history**. Since 2009, U.S. **agricultural exports have increased by roughly 53 percent**.

Agricultural Exports Continue to Grow

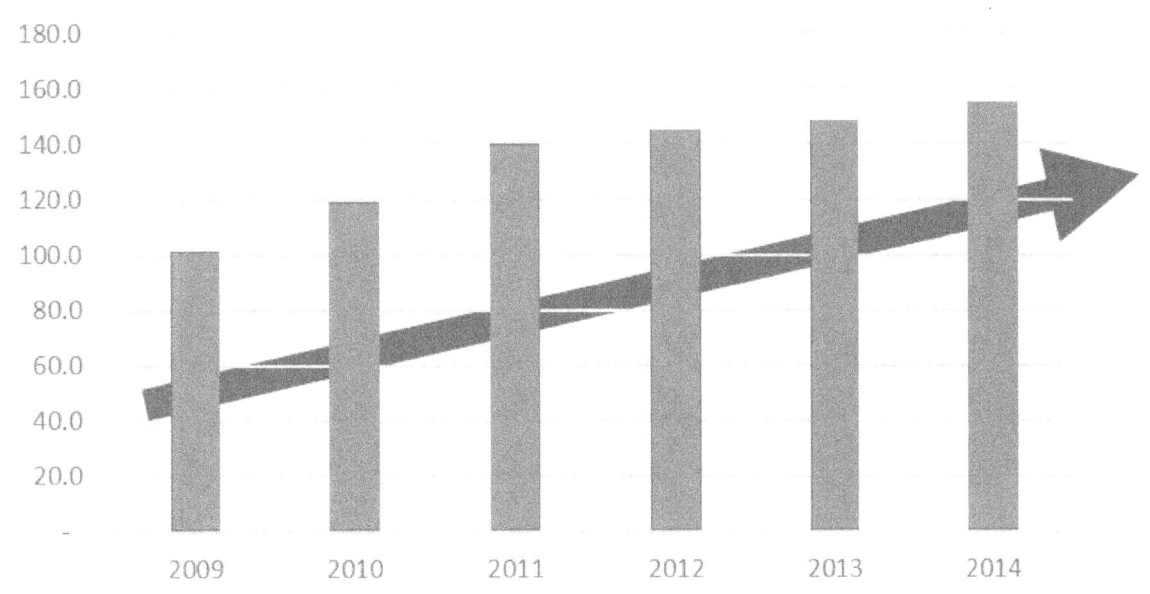

Exports are economically crucial to rural communities because **exports generate 20 percent of farm income** for U.S. agricultural producers and **support over a million American jobs**. In 2013, every dollar of agricultural exports stimulated another $1.22 in business activity.

The United States exports:

- Half of our wheat, milled rice, and soybean production
- 70 percent of our almonds, walnuts, and pistachios
- More than 75 percent of our cotton
- 40 percent of our grapes
- 20 percent of our apples
- 20 percent of our poultry and pork
- And 10 percent of our beef

Spotlight: Small Business

America's **28 million small businesses** are the backbone of the U.S. economy, and the primary engines of growth and innovation. Small businesses accounted for nearly two-third of new private sector jobs in recent decades, continued export growth for small businesses is a key priority. While **98 percent of U.S. all businesses that export are small businesses**, less than 10 percent of U.S. small businesses – around **300,000 small businesses – export**. That means we are well below our full small businesses exporting potential. **Small businesses that export grow faster, create more jobs, and pay higher wages**.

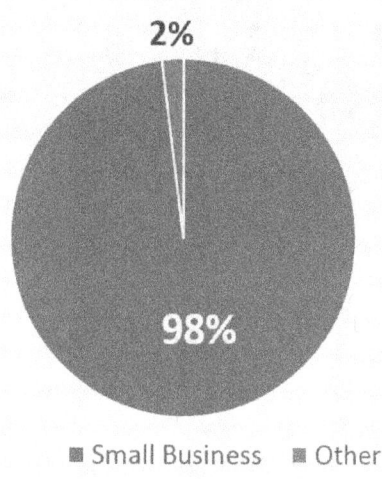

The trade agreements the Obama Administration is negotiating support small businesses by:

1. **Removing barriers to exports** by cutting tariffs and reducing non-tariff barriers.

2. **Simplifying trade** by including meaningful trade facilitation provisions, creating simplified and expedited customs rules, and applying strong and common rules of origin.

3. **Facilitating small business engagement** with global markets by promoting e-commerce and digital trade, and ensuring that provisions support SMEs.

Number of Small Business Exporters By State

State	Count	State	Count	State	Count
Alabama	3,229	Louisiana	3,378	Ohio	14,599
Alaska	438	Maine	1,857	Oklahoma	2,743
Arizona	6,946	Maryland	6,529	Oregon	5,289
Arkansas	1,758	Massachusetts	9,837	Pennsylvania	13,941
California	71,921	Michigan	13,535	Rhode Island	1,503
Colorado	4,900	Minnesota	7,564	South Carolina	5,091
Connecticut	5,232	Mississippi	1,535	South Dakota	731
Delaware	1,531	Missouri	5,100	Tennessee	5,958
Florida	58,976	Montana	1,385	Texas	37,921
Georgia	13,203	Nebraska	1,597	Utah	2,989
Hawaii	763	Nevada	2,437	Vermont	1,053
Idaho	1,463	New Hampshire	2,207	Virginia	6,542
Illinois	20,752	New Jersey	19,443	Washington	11,262
Indiana	6,995	New Mexico	1,062	West Virginia	861
Iowa	2,786	New York	38,675	Wisconsin	7,479
Kansas	2,830	North Carolina	9,299	Wyoming	363
Kentucky	3,634	North Dakota	1,669		

THE PRESIDENT'S TRADE POLICY PRIORITIES

1. Promote U.S. Interests and Values Through
   High Standard, Job-Supporting Trade

2. Enforce U.S. Trade Rights Around the World

3. Enhance Trade and Investment Relationships with
   Partners Worldwide

4. Fight Poverty and Foster Global Economic Growth Through
   Trade and Developoment

5. Inform the Public and Develop Balanced Trade Policy from
   Diverse Perspectives

Twenty-first century businesses, including small businesses, need to sell more American products overseas. Today, our businesses export more than ever, and exporters tend to pay their workers higher wages. But as we speak, China wants to write the rules for the world's fastest-growing region. That would put our workers and our businesses at a disadvantage. Why would we let that happen? We should write those rules. We should level the playing field. That's why I'm asking both parties to give me trade promotion authority to protect American workers, with strong new trade deals from Asia to Europe that aren't just free, but are also fair. It's the right thing to do.

Look, I'm the first one to admit that past trade deals haven't always lived up to the hype, and that's why we've gone after countries that break the rules at our expense. But 95 percent of the world's customers live outside our borders. We can't close ourselves off from those opportunities. More than half of manufacturing executives have said they're actively looking to bring jobs back from China. So let's give them one more reason to get it done.

Barack Obama
State of the Union
January 20, 2015

High Standard, Job-Supporting Trade Agreements

Trade's contribution to the U.S. economy has never been more significant than it is today. Trade supports higher-paying jobs, spurs economic growth, and enhances the competitiveness of the U.S. economy. Last year, the United States exported $2.35 trillion in goods and services, setting a new record for the fifth year in a row. Over the last five years, U.S. exports have accounted for nearly a third of total U.S. economic growth.

These economic gains pay real dividends for real people. Since 2009 under President Obama, U.S. exports have increased by nearly 50 percent, growing two and a half times faster than the economy as a whole, adding $762 billion dollars to our economic output and contributing nearly a third of our total economic growth.

Exports to countries we have free trade agreements with have significantly outpaced exports to countries where we do not have trade agreements.

Rising exports have been strengthening communities across America by supporting more high-paying jobs. Each billion dollars of increased exports supports over 5,000 jobs, on average. Between 2009 and 2014, exports supported an estimated 1.8 million additional private sector jobs – jobs that pay up to 18 percent more on average than non-export related jobs. Today, more than 300,000 American companies export, 98 percent of which are small and medium size businesses.

Trade agreements have played an important role in increasing U.S. exports. Over the past five years, exports of U.S. goods to our free trade agreement (FTA) partners increased over 64 percent, significantly outpacing the increase of around 45 percent to our non-FTA partners. Altogether, FTA partners accounted for nearly half of total U.S. goods exports to the world in 2014. Despite running an overall trade deficit, the United States runs a goods and services trade surplus with our combined 20 FTA partners. Our trade deficit, which has shrunk by a third since 2006, is comprised largely of the trade balance with our non-FTA partners.

The United States runs a trade surplus with our combined 20 trade agreement partners.

It's in our interest to build on this progress, because the United States is already an open economy. Our average applied tariff is less than 1.5 percent, among the lowest in the world, and we don't use regulations as a barrier to trade. America is open for business, but other countries still have real obstacles, tariff and non-tariff barriers, to our exports. As a result of that imbalance, our trade agreements disproportionately reduce other countries' barriers, allowing us to increase exports and the good-paying jobs they support. That's why it's essential for the United States to continue to pursue an ambitious trade agenda.

Spotlight: The Success of Existing Agreements

U.S. Trade Surplus with Free Trade Agreement Partners
(in $Billions, excluding energy products)

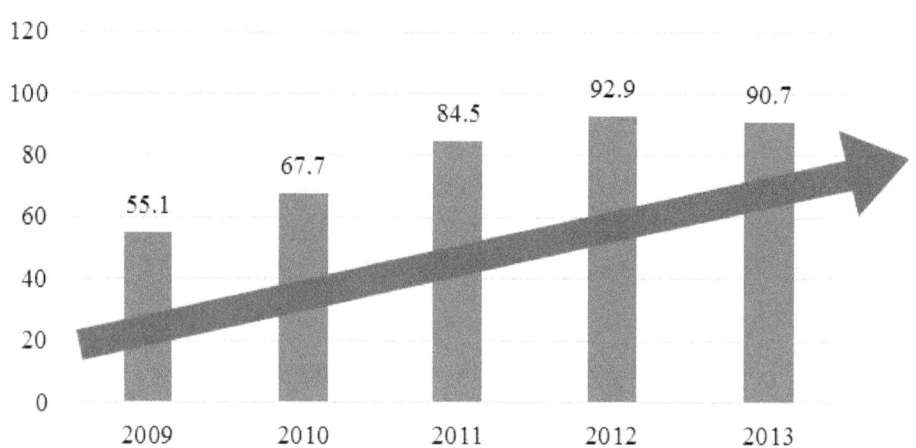

The U.S. has a trade surplus with our combined FTA partners.

This includes surpluses in services, manufacturing, and agriculture.

Sectoral Trade Surpluses with Free Trade Agreement Partners

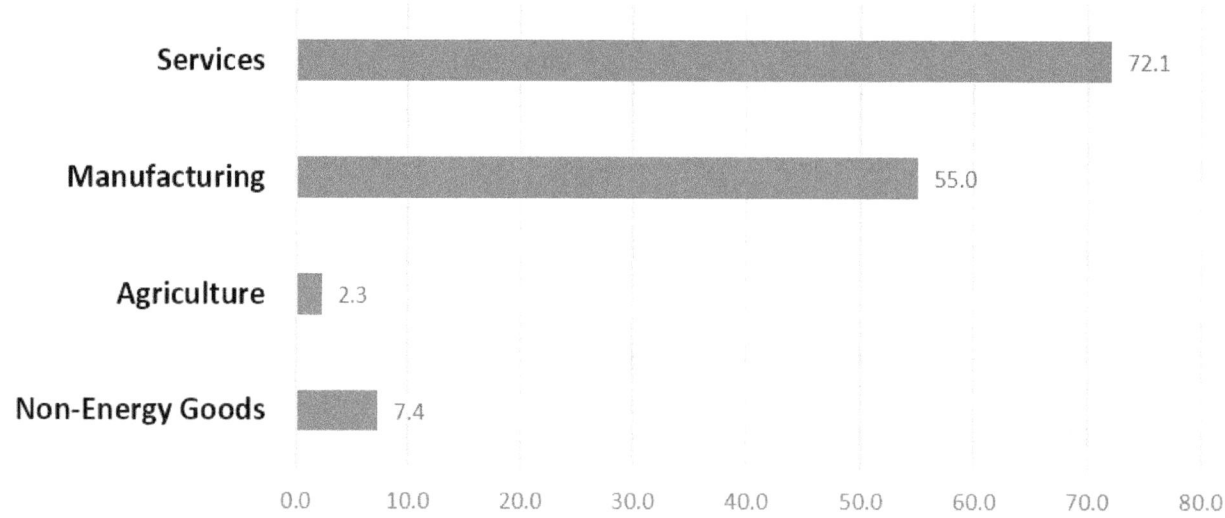

Our trade balance has improved with virtually all of our FTA partners since trade agreements went into force. Four (Bahrain, CAFTA-DR, Chile, and Colombia) have gone from deficit to surplus. Seven (Australia, Jordan, Morocco, Oman, Panama, Peru, and Singapore) have gone from surplus to larger surplus. We even have a growing surplus with NAFTA (excluding energy products, which are fundamentally unaffected by trade agreements). Our deficit with Korea has grown, but that is in large part due to slow economic growth in Korea. In 2014, U.S. exports to Korea increased 7 percent.

Worker Rights

To keep strengthening our economy, we need better trade rules that protect American jobs and workers. The Obama Administration believes that by improving labor rights through our trade initiatives abroad, we can simultaneously uphold and promote U.S. values, strengthen the ability of American workers here at home to have a fair shot at competing on a level playing field in the global marketplace, and help grow a larger middle class in our trading partners that will fuel demand for U.S. goods and services. The trade policy tools available to promote worker rights have evolved significantly over time. Twenty years ago, when the United States entered into NAFTA, labor provisions were secondary and not included in the core of the agreement. Rather, they were in a side agreement, virtually all of the provisions of which were not subject to any enforcement mechanism. Today, the Obama Administration is negotiating provisions that are fundamentally different from NAFTA – and at the core of the agreement, subject to dispute settlement and the full range of trade sanctions.

1994	NAFTA	Jordan	Singapore, Chile, Australia, Morocco, CAFTA-DR, Bahrain, Oman	Peru, Colombia, Korea, Panama	*2014* Trans-Pacific Partnership
Labor provisions in the core of the agreement.	✗	✓	✓	✓	✓
Parties must adopt and maintain fundamental labor rights	✗	✗	✗	✓	✓
Parties must not waive or derogate from laws implementing fundamental labor rights	✗	✗	✗	✓	✓
Parties must adopt and maintain statutes and regulations governing acceptable conditions of work	✗	✗	✗	✗	✓
Parties shall take measures to discourage importation of goods made by forced labor	✗	✗	✗	✗	✓
Parties shall not waive or derogate from *any* labor laws if it would weaken labor protections in export processing zones	✗	✗	✗	✗	✓
Parties must effectively enforce their own labor laws	✓	✓	✓	✓	✓
Normal dispute settlement applies to all labor provisions	✗	✓	✗	✓	✓
Normal trade sanctions apply to all labor provisions	✗	✓	✗	✓	✓

In 2015, we will seek to strengthen the respect for and protection of labor rights through our major trade negotiations. In TPP, we are negotiating to put in place the largest expansion of enforceable labor rights in history, renegotiating NAFTA and bringing hundreds of millions of additional people under enforceable International Labor Organization standards.

TPP is also providing a powerful avenue for direct engagement with countries like Vietnam, where because of TPP, we are making progress in improving the lives of workers on the ground. Under TPP, we are working to ensure that violations of labor rights will be subject to the same, strong dispute settlement mechanism as the rest of the commitments in the agreement. Some TPP countries will need to pursue reform so that their laws and practices are consistent with the International Labor Organization's fundamental labor rights. That includes freedom of association and the right to collective bargaining. It also includes protection from child and forced labor and from employment discrimination. Also, for the first time, we are seeking to include requirements in TPP for countries to adopt laws on minimum wages, hours of work, and occupational safety and health.

Just as the heart of America's economy is the American worker, the heart of the global economy should be working people who stand to share in the benefits of global growth. Along the same lines, we will use the unique opportunity afforded to us in T-TIP to negotiate obligations that protect worker rights and set a high bar for other trade negotiations in the rest of the world. More broadly, we will focus on the effectiveness of rule of law, implementation of the numerous agreements we have entered into, and work with key trading partners around the world to address specific labor issues.

Under the **Trans-Pacific Partnership** & the **Transatlantic Trade & Investment Partnership**

an estimated **649,762,600 workers**

in the combined free trade areas could benefit from the **strongest labor protections** in any trade agreement in history.

In addition, in 2015 we will aim to strengthen engagement on and monitoring of labor protections with a number of trading partners, in concert with other U.S. agencies and our partners in the labor movement:

- We will continue to engage with the governments of Colombia, Bangladesh, Guatemala, Honduras and the Dominican Republic to advance workers' rights.

- We will work with the Colombian government to advance the implementation of the Colombia Action Plan Related to Labor Rights, a critical component of the United States – Colombia Trade Promotion Agreement, and urge additional action on areas of concern such as collecting fines for unlawful subcontracting, targeting shifting forms of unlawful subcontracting, and prosecuting recent cases of violence against trade unionists.

- We will continue to consult with the government of Bangladesh to press for further progress on the GSP labor action plan, including issuing regulations implementing amendments to the Bangladesh Labour Act, completing building safety inspections, responding to unfair labor practice complaints, and enacting additional needed labor reforms, including for export processing zones.

- We will continue to engage with Guatemala following the September 2014 reactivation of our labor dispute settlement process.

- We will continue to press for improved labor conditions in Honduras and the Dominican Republic.

In each of these cases, we will continue to use our trade policy tools to ensure that workers are able to exercise their rights and to improve working conditions on the ground.

The heart of America's economy is the American worker.

Here at home, the Administration is committed to working with Congress to renew the Trade Adjustment Assistance (TAA) programs, which expired on December 31, 2013, to provide critical support for Americans facing short-term trade-related transitions. TAA provides resources to eligible workers to develop new skills that are essential for employment in vital growth industries of the 21st century economy. As the Obama Administration works hard to create and maintain open markets and support jobs through trade, we must also be mindful of our responsibility to ensure that trade policy reflects our values and stands with American workers impacted by global competition.

These goals are critical to the Administration's broader efforts to ensure a balanced, growing global economy in which workers in the United States and abroad share in the benefits of trade and globalization.

Environmental Protection

The Obama Administration is also working to set the world's highest standards in the environmental chapters of the trade agreements we are pursuing, and just like labor standards, we have insisted that environmental commitments be fully enforceable and on equal footing with commercial obligations. Through our TPP negotiations in particular, the Administration is seeking to address conservation challenges that are particularly prevalent in the Asia-Pacific region. We have insisted that environmental protections be at the core of TPP, and be enforceable through the same type of dispute settlement as other obligations, including the availability of trade sanctions. Our TPP partners include five of the world's most biologically diverse countries, and encompass major consumer and export markets for threatened and endangered wildlife. Of the estimated $70-213 billion dollars in wildlife trafficking and related environmental crime that takes place annually, an estimated $8-10 billion dollars in illegal trade takes place in South-East Asia alone.

In TPP we are pressing for groundbreaking and enforceable obligations to combat wildlife trafficking, and because TPP encompasses some of the world's major markets for wildlife and wildlife products, these efforts will potentially make all the difference for endangered and iconic species like rhinos and elephants, as well as reptiles, tropical birds and fish. TPP also presents an opportunity to advance protections for our oceans. TPP partners include eight of the world's top 20 fishing nations, accounting for 30 percent of global marine catch and almost 25 percent of global seafood exports. And TPP will also help protect forests and combat illegal logging. TPP countries account for over 30 percent of global timber and pulp production, and Malaysia alone is the largest exporter of tropical timber products in the world. TPP creates a significant opportunity to step up regional efforts to effectively enforce conservation laws, better coordinate law enforcement efforts, combat illegal logging, and target capacity building to promote sustainable timber management schemes.

The Obama Administration is working to set the world's highest environmental standards in the trade agreements it is negotiating.

In 2015, we will also continue to monitor closely the implementation of environmental obligations under existing trade agreements. For example, we will continue our engagement with Peru on its recent economic reforms to emphasize to the Peruvian government that the reforms must not weaken environmental protection. We will also continue to work with Peru to support its implementation of the Annex on Forest Sector Governance and the January 2013 bilateral Action Plan targeting key challenges in Peru's forestry sector.

This year at the WTO, we will continue to work with the world's largest traders of environmental goods to eliminate tariffs on these products through the EGA negotiations. These negotiations commenced on July 8, 2014 and, in addition to the United States, include Australia, Canada, China, Costa Rica, the European Union, Hong Kong, Israel, Japan, Korea, New Zealand, Norway, Singapore, Switzerland, Chinese Taipei and Turkey – together accounting for more than 87 percent of global trade in environmental goods. Iceland is also planning to join in 2015. The EGA will build on the commitment that President Obama and other Leaders of the Asia-Pacific Economic Cooperation (APEC) made to reduce tariffs on a list of 54 environmental goods and will expand product coverage to include additional environmental technologies. Eliminating tariffs on goods that help us protect our environment, such as renewable and clean energy technologies, will make these technologies both more affordable and accessible.

Innovation and Creativity

The United States is a leading voice for strong intellectual property rights protection that promotes incentives for innovation in place, while ensuring access to medicine for the world's poor. The Obama Administration strongly believes that our trade agreements should reflect this principle. For example, we are working to develop an approach in TPP that has a strong pharmaceutical IP standard, but that allows for more tailored flexibility for developing countries. We will continue to work with TPP partners in 2015 to make life-saving medicines more widely available, while maintaining incentives for the development of new treatments and cures.

The United States is a leading voice for strong intellectual property rights protection.

As global commerce evolves to include an expanded role for the digital economy, the Obama Administration will continue to work towards strengthening America's competitive advantage in innovation. Intellectual property (IP) serves the essential purpose of encouraging innovation and creativity, and with over 40 million Americans employed in IP-intensive industries, it is an important source of American jobs. To sustain these vital economic benefits, in 2015 the United States will continue to seek greater market access for IP-intensive U.S. products, and to promote job-supporting innovation and creativity with balanced policies that benefit both producers and users of innovative products and services. The Administration will continue to work with the negotiating partners and stakeholders to advance high-standard IP provisions that will protect and promote the spread of IP-intensive products and services in major trade initiatives like TPP, T-TIP, and will advance positive discussions of trade-related innovation and related issues at the World Trade Organization in Geneva.

We will continue to seek greater market access for IP-intensive U.S. products – and to defend the millions of American jobs threatened by the theft of U.S. intellectual property.

As we work to open new markets to innovations from American firms, the U.S. will aggressively defend millions of American jobs threatened by the wholesale theft of U.S. intellectual property. Our workers deserve to reap the benefits of their labor, and we will use all appropriate trade policy tools to address key trade-related IP issues and resolve specific intellectual property issues that undermine the rights of Americans. We seek to actively combat global counterfeiting that both threatens American jobs and often endangers the health and safety of global consumers. We will also continue to advance the interests of U.S. producers, including trademark holders and exporters that rely on the use of generic product names, against over-broad protection of geographical indications in foreign markets.

The United States will continue to use the "Special 301" process and resulting annual report to Congress to drive continued improvements to the IPR protection and enforcement systems of our trading partners and to address ongoing foreign market access challenges facing our IP-intensive industries. The 2014 Special 301 Report marked 25 years of this Congressionally-mandated review, throughout which USTR has identified positive advances as well as areas of continued concern, reflected changing technologies, promoted best practices, and situated these critical issues in their policy context. The Report will continue to underscore the economic benefits of intellectual property rights protection and enforcement to the United States and to our trading partners and the need for our trading partners to comply with their international intellectual property obligations. For instance, in 2015 we expect to review and report on critical developments in key markets such as China, Russia and India, all named as Priority Watch List countries in 2014.

As with the rest of our trade agenda, the Administration will continue to seek input from Congress and stakeholders on a wide range of trade issues related to the protection and enforcement of copyrights, trademarks, patents, trade secrets, and other forms of intellectual property. In the area of public health, the Administration continues to welcome diverse stakeholder input to shape the development of proposals to promote access to high-quality innovative and generic medical products.

The Trans-Pacific Partnership

The Obama Administration will work to conclude negotiations of the Trans-Pacific Partnership (TPP) in 2015. TPP will include the strongest labor and environmental provisions of any trade agreement, as well as new provisions that create disciplines on state-owned enterprises, advance digital freedom, promote the development of and access to innovation, strengthen anticorruption efforts, benefit small businesses, and further global development. TPP is integral to the U.S. rebalance to Asia and allows us to set the rules of the road in an important and dynamic region – rules that will otherwise be set by countries that do not share our interests or our values.

TPP will level the playing field for American workers and businesses in the world's fastest growing region.

The 12 TPP partners – the United States, as well as Australia, Brunei Darussalam, Canada, Chile, Japan, Malaysia, Mexico, New Zealand, Peru, Singapore, and Vietnam – are responsible for nearly 40 percent of the global economy and one-third of global trade. These large and growing markets are already key destinations for U.S. manufactured goods, agricultural products, and services, and the TPP will further deepen this trade and investment relationship while promoting our values. TPP will level the playing field for American workers and businesses in the world's fastest-growing region. At present, American autoworkers are handicapped by tariffs that can reach 30 percent in rapidly growing markets such as Malaysia. American farmers are forced to contend with tariffs as high as 40 percent on poultry in Vietnam. In these industries and others, TPP will eliminate or significantly reduce barriers to U.S. exports.

In addition, the United States continues to engage with potential candidate countries regarding their interest in joining the TPP negotiations in the future and has welcomed public expressions of interest by a number of economies in Asia and Latin America. TPP remains a promising platform for the development of a global trading system based on U.S. values and rules that enhance public health and consumer safety.

The Transatlantic Trade and Investment Partnership

T-TIP will build on what is already the world's largest trade and investment relationship, between the United States and the European Union.

The United States and the European Union already share the largest trade and investment relationship in the world with $1 trillion in two-way annual trade (an average of $2.7 billion each day). T-TIP will build on that. With the new European Commission in place, the United States and the European Union are seeking to build on that strong foundation, and are moving forward with a fresh start in the T-TIP negotiations. Last November, President Obama and EU leaders reaffirmed their commitment to an ambitious, comprehensive, and high-standard T-TIP agreement.

In 2015, the Administration expects to make substantial progress in the T-TIP negotiations. We are seeking ambitious market openings in goods, services, and investment, and are working to address areas such as regulatory and other non-tariff barriers to U.S. exports, increasing the participation of SMEs in the transatlantic economy, and addressing the challenges of trade in the modern digital economy, among other goals.

T-TIP offers the United States an historic opportunity to modernize trade rules and break down barriers between our two markets. We will do so in a way that maintains the high levels of protection for consumers, for health and safety, for the environment, and for workers that our citizens expect. It also offers significant opportunities to set high standards with respect to global issues of common concern, beyond the bilateral U.S.-EU relationship. And in addition to the economic benefits, T-TIP will reinforce the crucial strategic elements of our transatlantic relationship. The Administration will continue to seek input from Congress and a wide variety of stakeholders as the T-TIP negotiations progress.

Building on Success in TPP

Goods

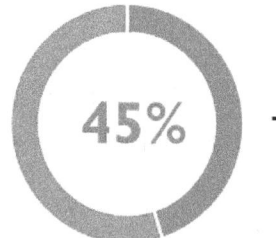 **45%**

$727 billion
U.S. goods exports to TPP countries in 2014: 45% of all U.S. goods exports

Manufacturing

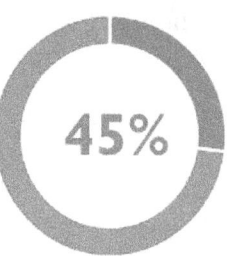 **45%**

$638 billion
U.S. manufacturing exports to TPP countries in 2014: 45% of all U.S. manufacturing exports

Agriculture

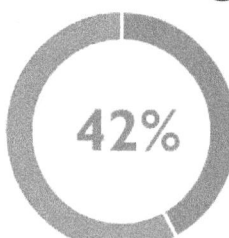 **42%**

$66 billion
U.S. agriculture exports to TPP countries in 2014: 42% of all U.S. agricultural exports

Services

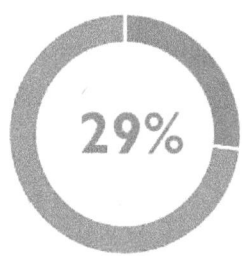 **29%**

$199 billion
U.S. services exports to TPP countries in 2013: 29% of all U.S. services exports

1.5 million U.S. workers
employed by companies headquartered in TPP countries

Building on Success in T-TIP

Goods

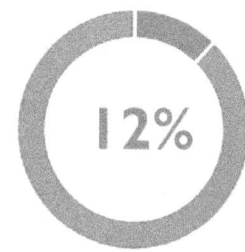 **12%**

$277 billion
U.S. goods exports to T-TIP countries in 2014: 12% of all U.S. goods exports

Manufacturing

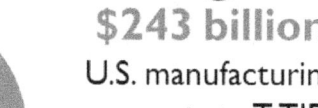 **45%**

$243 billion
U.S. manufacturing exports to T-TIP countries in 2014: 17% of all U.S. manufacturing exports

Agriculture

8%

$13 billion
U.S. agriculture exports to T-TIP countries in 2014: 8% of all U.S. agricultural exports

Services

 **30%**

$206 billion
U.S. services exports to T-TIP countries in 2013: 30% of all U.S. services exports

3.3 million U.S. workers
employed by companies headquartered in T-TIP countries

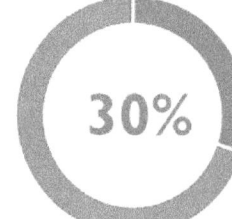

Information Technology and Services

The United States will continue to play a leading role in negotiations to expand the scope of products covered by the Information Technology Agreement (ITA) within the WTO framework. The ITA entered into force in 1997 and now covers over $4 trillion in annual global trade. The Obama Administration is seeking to expand the scope of the ITA's product coverage in order to keep pace with the tremendous technological advances that have taken place in recent years. Following the 2014 APEC Leaders' Meeting, President Obama announced a major breakthrough

with China, which allowed the plurilateral negotiations to expand the scope of goods covered by the ITA to continue. A plurilateral deal on ITA expansion will eliminate tariffs on additional information technology products, and would be the first major tariff deal at the WTO in 18 years.

In 2015, U.S. negotiators will work to conclude negotiations on a balanced and commercially meaningful expansion of the ITA. Eliminating duties on newer information technology products would provide a significant boost for U.S. technology exports, and enable all countries to benefit from increased trade of cutting edge products. The Information Technology and Innovation Foundation estimates that the liberalization of duties on additional technology products could increase annual global GDP by $190 billion and support up to 60,000 new American jobs.

In order to strengthen our leadership position as a global supplier of services, in 2014, the Administration held five rounds of negotiations for a Trade in Services Agreement (TiSA) to open foreign markets, create new opportunities for U.S. exporters, and encourage the adoption of policies that promote fair and open competition in international markets for services. Twenty-three economies participated in TiSA negotiations in 2014, representing 75 percent of the world's $44 trillion services market – or approximately half of the global economy. This year we will continue to advance negotiations on TiSA, and hope to achieve substantial progress towards reaching an agreement.

World Trade Organization

The World Trade Organization remains the critical forum for strengthening the multilateral rules-based trading system and enforcing global trade rules, while serving as an important bulwark against protectionism.

In 2015, the United States will build on recent multilateral trade negotiating successes by continuing to play a leading role in the multilateral trading system. This leadership role reflects our commitment to preserving, enhancing, and strengthening the WTO as an institution going forward. Earlier this year, the Administration took the final step towards enabling full implementation of the WTO Trade Facilitation Agreement, the first multilateral trade agreement in the WTO's 20-year history. This hard won agreement promises to improve trade efficiency and help small businesses export, and is projected to generate hundreds of billions of dollars in economic activity. The WTO TFA, with binding commitments on all WTO Members to expedite movement, release and clearance of goods, improve cooperation on customs matters, and help developing countries fully implement the obligations, will open new markets for U.S. exporters by significantly reducing customs barriers they face worldwide. The agreement will increase customs efficiency and effective collection of revenue, and will help small businesses access new export opportunities through requirements for transparency in customs practices, reduction of documentary requirements, and processing of documents before goods arrive.

In 2015, the United States will seize upon this forward momentum by encouraging other WTO members to take the necessary steps so that the entry-into-force of the TFA occurs by the 10th Ministerial Conference in Kenya in December. We will also establish, with our partners at USAID, an innovative public-private partnership to provide capacity-building assistance to select developing countries that demonstrate strong commitments to rapidly implement the TFA.

The WTO remains the critical forum for strengthening the multilateral rules-based trading system and enforcing global trade rules, while serving as an important bulwark against protectionism.

The United States is once again playing a lead role in resuming a discussion with WTO members to conclude the Doha Round of global trade negotiations. Initial discussions in early 2014 on this "post-Bali work program" immediately faced many of the same challenges that have affected the Doha Agenda since its inception in 2001, including questions regarding the willingness of advanced developing countries to contribute commensurate to their status as major traders. This year, as these difficult discussions progress, we will continue to push the ultimate goal of the Round, which is to reduce trade barriers in order to expand global economic growth, development, and opportunity.

The United States also looks forward to the completion of several important WTO accession negotiations, including Kazakhstan (where we are working to ensure that measures in the Eurasian Economic Union are WTO consistent), Liberia (as it seeks to strengthen its economy while emerging from the Ebola crisis), and Afghanistan (as we continue to assist with the Afghan government's state-building efforts). The United States will continue to provide technical and other assistance to other WTO accession candidates.

While supporting the expansion of WTO membership and playing a proactive role in market-opening negotiations, we will continue to promote and strengthen the WTO's existing core functions, including the day-to-day activities of the WTO committees and working groups and the dispute settlement mechanism. These institutional structures are critical to promoting transparency in WTO Member trade policies, as well as monitoring and resisting protectionist pressures during a challenging time for certain segments of the global economy. By working together, WTO Members can continue to build upon 2014's successful efforts to revitalize the WTO and ensure that it remains equipped to drive future economic growth and development by serving as a permanent bulwark against protectionist measures around the world.

Trade Enforcement

The Obama Administration is committed to vigilant monitoring and rigorous enforcement of U.S. trade rights. Our enforcement efforts are essential to growing our economy and defending the livelihoods of hard-working Americans. It is for this reason that President Obama has placed trade enforcement on par with opening markets for U.S. exports. The United States will use every appropriate tool at our disposal to fight a variety of unjust trade barriers to ensure that the rights of America's working families are fully realized.

In 2015, the Obama Administration will continue to use dialogue when possible – and WTO dispute settlement when necessary – to help preserve and support American jobs threatened by foreign practices inconsistent with the obligations of our trade agreements and at the WTO. As we continue to defend and enforce U.S. trade rights, our goal remains to ensure that Americans can compete successfully in world markets where intellectual property is protected, labor and environmental standards are enforced, where regulations to protect human, animal, or plant life or health are based on science and where transparent rules and regulations are applied without discrimination.

The Obama Administration is committed to vigilant monitoring and rigorous enforcement of U.S. trade rights. Our enforcement efforts are essential to growing our economy and defending the livelihoods of hard-working Americans.

The WTO's dispute settlement system plays an indispensable role as the preeminent forum for the discussion and adjudication of disputes with our trading partners. The United States prevailed in four major WTO disputes in 2014, successfully challenging China's export restraints on rare earths elements, China's antidumping and countervailing duties on U.S. automobiles, Argentina's sweeping import licensing restrictions, and India's ban on imports of various U.S. agricultural products like poultry meat, eggs, and live swine. These successful outcomes are clear examples of the Administration's winning strategy of fighting back against countries that unfairly block or discriminate against U.S. exports or distort trade against U.S. interests.

As a top priority in 2015, we will continue to hold China and other trade partners accountable to their WTO obligations to ensure that U.S. producers and workers have a level playing field to compete in a wide range of industries. This Administration is dedicated to ensuring that

Americans get the benefits of all the economic opportunities we've negotiated under our trade agreements. For example, last month we launched a new enforcement action against China's "Demonstration Bases-Common Service Platform" export subsidy program. Under this questionable program, China seems to provide prohibited export subsidies through "Common Service Platforms" to manufacturers and producers across seven economic sectors and dozens of sub-sectors located in more than one hundred and fifty industrial clusters throughout China known as "Demonstration Bases." This unfair Chinese program is harmful to American workers and American businesses of all sizes, and we are dedicated to combatting these unfair practices.

Going forward this year, the United States will also continue to pursue ongoing WTO disputes, including three WTO actions launched in 2014. Specifically, we will continue to fight against barriers to U.S. products, whether China's antidumping and countervailing duties on imports of U.S. electrical steel; Indonesia's licensing measures that restrict imports of American horticultural and animal products; or India's domestic content requirements for solar cells and solar modules that discriminate against American manufacturers.

In addition, in 2015, the United States will continue to pursue meaningful efforts with the EU to end WTO-inconsistent subsidies for aircraft at the earliest possible date. Tens of thousands of jobs for U.S. aerospace engineers, electricians, and related suppliers depend on U.S. aircraft manufacturers being able to compete globally on a level playing field. At the same time, the United States is vigorously defending U.S. interests in the compliance challenge brought by the EU.

> *The United States will fight against barriers to U.S. products, whether China's antidumping and countervailing duties on imports of U.S. electrical steel or India's domestic content requirements for solar products that discriminate against American manufacturers.*

In 2015, the Interagency Trade Enforcement Center (ITEC) will continue to play a critical role in the Obama Administration's enforcement efforts. ITEC brings together resources and expertise from across the federal government into one unit organization reporting to the USTR. ITEC includes staff from a variety of agencies with a diverse set of language skills and expertise, including intellectual property rights, subsidy analysis, economics, agriculture, and animal health science. This collaborative structure is significantly enhancing the Administration's capacity to proactively enforce U.S. trade rights. For example, through ITEC the United States will continue to push farther and dig deeper into, and address trade distortions resulting from, the complex web of industrial policies and bureaucratic systems of key trading partners like China. Furthermore, ITEC will continually monitor compliance of other key trading partners, such as Russia, Brazil and India, with their WTO commitments and on priority issues like distortive industrial policies, localization policies and IPR, in coordination with trade experts from across the U.S. government.

Building on the achievements of the last four years, in 2015 we will continue to work with Korea, Colombia, and Panama to ensure that the bilateral trade agreements that went into effect in 2012 are fully implemented and continue to operate smoothly. Moving forward in 2015, the United States and Korea will jointly convene relevant committees and working groups established under the agreement as necessary to ensure continuing implementation of its provisions.

Spotlight: Labor Enforcement

Guatemala

We are engaged in a formal dispute settlement process, having exhausted consultative efforts aimed at ensuring that workers are afforded the protections they are due under Guatemalan labor law. As the first Administration to make use of such a mechanism, the Obama Administration has made clear that the objective is not punitive, but rather to ensure that Guatemala upholds the commitments it has made under the CAFTA-DR with respect to workers' rights.

Bahrain

We have pursued formal consultations under the United States-Bahrain agreement to address concerns regarding targeting of union leaders in the events surrounding the 2011 Arab Spring civil unrest. Bahrain has made important progress, such as reinstating the vast majority of workers who had been dismissed in that process, but significant challenges remain and USTR and DOL are continuing to engage to try to resolve them.

Colombia

A long and constructive engagement with the Government led to the negotiation of the extensive Colombian Action Plan Related to Labor Right. This plan was designed to address longstanding concerns relating to violence against labor leaders, impunity for such acts and protection of labor rights. The two countries have worked closely on implementation of the plan, drawing on strong engagement by stakeholders in both countries. Important progress has been made but much more work remains.

Jordan

Our engagement has produced an Implementation Plan Related to Working and Living Conditions of Workers that is helping to address concerns about workers' rights and working conditions in Jordan's garment sector, particularly with respect to foreign workers. Jordan has issued new standards for dormitory inspections, submitted new labor legislation to its parliament and hired new labor inspectors. The ILO has been an important partner and has ramped up its engagement to support protections for foreign workers in Jordan.

Bangladesh, Swaziland, and Haiti

The Administration has been using the tools in U.S. preference programs to protect labor rights. Each of these countries is eligible for benefits under different programs— Bangladesh from the Generalized System of Preferences (GSP), Swaziland from the African Growth and Opportunity Act (AGOA) and HOPE program for Haiti. These programs all condition preferential market access on meeting certain "eligibility criteria," which include criteria relating to labor rights. While the specific labor criteria in each program are unique, the Obama Administration has made use of all of them to address a range of serious problems: from lack of worker voice, to building and fire safety concerns, to acts of violence and intimidation towards union organizers, to employment-related sexual harassment. Addressing these issues is not only critical to protecting workers' rights, it is necessary for strengthening developing countries' growth strategies.

Spotlight: China Enforcement

Presidential Safeguard Action on Tires from China. In September 2009, President Obama directed the imposition for three years of additional tariffs to stop a harmful surge of imports of Chinese tires for passenger cars and light trucks. The surge caused production of U.S. tires to drop, domestic tire plants to close, and Americans to lose their jobs. Acting on behalf of American manufacturers and workers, President Obama invoked a law that had been passed but never before used to give the United States the right under WTO rules to address harm caused by imports from China. The President's action was subsequently upheld by the WTO, which rejected in its entirety a challenge by China to the action.

Chinese AD/CVD Duties on Autos from the United States. In July 2012, the United States challenged China's anti-dumping and countervailing duties on certain automobiles from the United States. The WTO agreed with the United States that China's duties breached numerous international trade rules. Following the U.S. challenge and before issuance of the panel's report, China announced the termination of its AD and CVD duties. In 2013, those duties had been imposed on exports of over $5 billion of American-made cars and sport-utility vehicles (SUVs). Through this dispute, the Administration is ensuring the right of American companies to fair treatment in antidumping and countervailing duty investigations in China.

Export Restraints on Rare Earths. In March 2012, the United States challenged China's export restraints on rare earths, tungsten and molybdenum products. China is the world's leading producer of rare earths, producing an estimated 130,000 metric tons of rare earth oxide, which accounted for approximately 97 percent of global production in 2011. In all, China's export restraints on the materials at issue in this dispute cover approximately 100 tariff codes. The United States brought this dispute to create a level playing field for U.S. workers and businesses that manufacture many important downstream products in the United States, including hybrid car batteries, wind turbines, energy-efficient lighting, steel, advanced electronics, automobiles, petroleum and chemicals. In late 2014, the WTO agreed with the United States and found that China's export restraints are inconsistent with WTO rules. China has until May 2015 to comply.

Export Restraints on Raw Materials. In June 2009, the United States challenged China's export restraints on nine raw materials to create a level playing field for U.S. workers and businesses that manufacture downstream products in the steel, aluminum and chemical sectors. The case addressed a main problem: the export restraints enabled China's downstream producers to obtain a dramatic competitive advantage by significantly decreasing their input costs. For example, in 2008, the input cost for coke was 36 percent less for Chinese domestic steel producers than their foreign counterparts. In 2011, the WTO found China's quotas and duties to be inconsistent with its WTO commitments. In December 2012, China eliminated the offending measures.

Chinese AD/CVD Duties on High Tech Steel from the United States. In September 2010, the United States challenged China's imposition of antidumping (AD) and countervailing duties (CVD) against U.S. exports of grain oriented flat-rolled electrical steel (GOES). This action cut off more than $250 million in U.S. exports of this high-tech steel product. In July 2012, the WTO found China's measures to be inconsistent with its WTO commitments. In 2014, the United States challenged China's failure to comply with the WTO. That dispute is ongoing.

Electronic Payment Services. In September 2010, the United States challenged China's restrictions and requirements on electronic payment services (EPS) for payment card transactions and the suppliers of those services. Each year well over one $1 trillion worth of electronic payment card transactions are processed in China. In 2012, the WTO agreed with the United States that China's measures discriminate against U.S. suppliers. China has taken some steps to address the problems identified by the WTO, and the Administration continues to work with U.S. stakeholders and China to ensure American credit and debit card companies' fair access to China's market.

Wind Power Equipment. In December 2010, following a petition from the United Steelworkers, the United States initiated a WTO case challenging subsidies that China provided to manufacturers in its wind power equipment sector. The subsidies appeared to require the use of local content, at the expense of foreign manufacturers' products. At the time of the dispute, grants provided under this program from 2008 to 2010 totaled several hundred million dollars. In response to our challenge, China terminated the challenged subsidy program.

Chinese AD/CVD Duties on Poultry from the United States. In September 2011, the United States challenged China's AD/CVD duties on U.S. exports of chicken "broiler products." According to industry estimates at the time, the U.S. poultry industry stood to lose approximately $1 billion in sales to China by the end 2011. In June 2013, the WTO agreed that China's measures were inconsistent with its WTO commitments. China issued a new measure in response to the WTO finding in 2014. The United States is reviewing that measure.

Chinese Export Bases for Autos and Auto Parts. In September 2012, the United States challenged a Chinese export subsidies program to auto and auto parts enterprises in China that severely distort competition. In the years 2002 through 2011, the value of China's exports of autos and auto parts increased more than nine-fold, from $7.4 billion to $69.1 billion, and China rose from the world's 16th largest to the 5th largest auto and auto parts exporter during this period. The United States was in a position to challenge these subsidies as a result of the critical investigative and analytical resources provided by the Interagency Trade Enforcement Center. Our efforts to address this important program are ongoing.

China Demonstration Bases for Common Service Platform. On February 11, 2015, the United States announced the decision to pursue dispute settlement consultations with the Government of China at the World Trade Organization (WTO) concerning China's "Demonstration Bases-Common Service Platform" export subsidy program. Under this questionable program, China seems to have provided $1 billion over 3 years to "Common Service Platforms" to give discounted or free services to Chinese companies including those in the seven economic sectors and dozens of sub-sectors located in more than one hundred and fifty industrial clusters throughout China known as "Demonstration Bases." This unfair Chinese program is harmful to American workers and American businesses of all sizes. Over two million U.S. workers are employed in the industries that compete with those that China supports through its Demonstration Base-Common Service Platform program.

Engagement with Key Trading Partners

Trade plays a leading role as a tool for strengthening bilateral and regional partnerships. The United States continues to promote mutual accountability and shared ambition as we work to strengthen our trade relationships and support U.S. jobs through a variety of bilateral and regional trade and investment avenues. In addition to our ongoing major negotiations with partners in Asia, Europe, and around the world, in 2015 the United States will maintain steady engagement with trading partners to create additional bilateral and regional trade and investment opportunities that help grow our economy.

China

President Obama is committed to robust U.S. engagement with China that focuses on providing American businesses with a level playing field to compete in China's large and growing market. Moving forward, the Obama Administration will seek to enhance cooperation toward common objectives on the basis of our shared responsibility to sustain global economic growth and stability.

Our efforts to promote healthy and equitable trade and investment with China will build on recent progress in several areas. Bilateral engagement in 2014 through the Joint Commission on Commerce and Trade (JCCT) and the Strategic and Economic Dialogue (S&ED) was productive, though there is more work ahead of us. At the JCCT in Chicago, we announced key outcomes in the areas of agricultural market access, intellectual property rights protection and related regulatory reforms, innovation policies, and competition law enforcement. And at the S&ED, the United States and China underscored the importance of fostering an open, transparent, and non-discriminatory environment for trade and investment on issues related to state owned enterprises, trade secrets, excess production capacity, and many others.

In 2015, we will pursue our trade and investment objectives with China using all available tools, including dialogue, negotiation, and enforcement when appropriate as we seek to eliminate market access barriers, ensure the unencumbered exercise of intellectual property rights, and increase transparency across all sectors. We will continue concrete steps to make maximum progress in Bilateral Investment Treaty (BIT) negotiations with China, consistent with our negative list approach and a commitment to national treatment in the pre-establishment phase. We will continue to work towards securing China's participation in the Government Procurement Agreement (GPA) to support rebalancing of the U.S.-China trade relationship by expanding U.S. sales into China's large government procurement market. We will work with China to improve intellectual property protection, to remove regulatory barriers, and to improve time-to-market of innovative pharmaceuticals and medical devices in China.

Korea

Last year, the United States and Korea held a number of bilateral trade consultations, including FTA committee meetings and working groups under the U.S.-Korea Free Trade Agreement to ensure full implementation of commitments made under the agreement. The United States raised and resolved a number of concerns, including in the automotive, financial services, and customs areas. In 2015, The United States will continue these consultations to address bilateral trade issues in a timely fashion. The United States and Korea will also continue to cooperate extensively in a range of multilateral and regional fora, such as APEC and the Trade in Services Agreement (TiSA).

Russia

In 2014, Russia's use of unjustified and retaliatory trade measures rejected the core principle of trade based on the rule of law. The Obama Administration responded to Russia's illegal actions in Ukraine by politically isolating and imposing economic costs on Russia through a carefully constructed sanctions regime, in close cooperation with Europe and other partners. We will continue to monitor Russia's implementation of its WTO obligations through USTR's annual reports detailing Russia's compliance, and take any actions necessary to ensure U.S. exports are treated consistently with those commitments.

India

Increasing trade and investment between the United States and India is critical to enhancing the dynamism of this important economic relationship. Two-way U.S.-India trade in goods in 1980 was just $2.8 billion; since then it has skyrocketed to $66.9 billion. In 2014, India hosted the eighth ministerial-level meeting of the India-United States Trade Policy Forum (TPF) in New Delhi. The two governments signaled their readiness to enhance bilateral trade and investment ties in a manner that promotes economic growth and job creation in both India and the United States and exchanged views on a range of issues, including agriculture, services, promoting investment in manufacturing, and intellectual property. Both India and the United States agreed upon TPF work plans for continued engagement in these areas in 2015. At the direction of the President and Prime Minister, we also plan to discuss the prospects for moving forward with a high-standard BIT as India releases its model BIT. In addition, we aim to achieve substantial progress on intellectual property issues with India through the High Level Working Group on Intellectual Property.

The Americas

The United States maintains strong economic ties with its trading partners throughout the Western Hemisphere. Boasting a combined goods and services trade totaling nearly $2 trillion, we seek to build upon an extensive web of existing bilateral and regional trade agreements to further enhance U.S. export opportunities to the region. With regard to Mexico, in 2014 we took further steps to deepen our economic partnership through the High Level Economic Dialogue. In

2015, we will continue to work bilaterally, and as TPP partners, to deepen our partnerships, enhance North American competitiveness, and address barriers to U.S. exports.

In October 2014, the United States and Brazil signed a Memorandum of Understanding (MOU) to permanently end the WTO cotton dispute, eliminating a longstanding irritant in our bilateral relationship. Under the terms of the MOU, Brazil formally terminated the WTO dispute and gave up its right to introduce countermeasures against U.S. trade or initiate any further proceedings in the dispute. In 2015, we will work to continue to grow our exports and deepen our trade and investment policy engagement with Brazil through the Agreement on Trade and Economic Cooperation (ATEC). We will also work to deepen our trade with our other FTA partners in South America, Chile, Peru and Colombia. All covered goods trade with Chile is now duty free, and we are working with both Chile and Peru as partners in the TPP.

Trade between the United States and Central America and the Caribbean remains strong. U.S. goods exports to the CAFTA-DR countries were valued at $31.3 billion in 2014. In 2015, the United States will work to deepen trade its relationships with CAFTA-DR partners to strengthen implementation of the trade agreement, facilitate trade and address outstanding issues related to IP, SPS measures, worker rights, and environmental protections, among others. Most of the Caribbean enjoys preferential access to the United States through our only permanent preference program, known as the Caribbean Basin Initiative. In 2015, we will continue our engagement with the region to encourage even greater trade and investment. And conditional on action by the U.S. Congress, actions in the Caribbean region could also include steps to re-establish normal trade relations with Cuba.

Sub-Saharan Africa

The U.S. will also intensify engagement with trading partners in sub-Saharan Africa to advance key trade and investment initiatives. As President Obama emphasized at the U.S.-Africa Business Forum on the margins of the U.S.-Africa Leaders Summit in August 2014, Africa includes some of the fastest-growing economies in the world, with a growing middle class and expanding markets in manufacturing, retail, and telecommunications. U.S. companies increasingly see opportunities in Africa, and we are working to support increased U.S.-Africa trade through the Trade Africa initiative as well as the long-term renewal of AGOA. We will work with Congress on a seamless and timely renewal of the AGOA program, which is scheduled to expire in September 30, 2015, for as long a term as possible.

We aim to significantly advance President Obama's Trade Africa Initiative through our work with the East African Community (EAC) in facilitating U.S.-EAC private sector engagement, by expanding the program to include additional countries, and by utilizing expanded trade and investment hubs across Africa to support U.S. investors and local businesses. At the U.S.-Africa Leaders Summit the President announced $7 billion in new financing to support U.S. exports to Africa as well as the creation of the President's Advisory Council on Doing Business in Africa. Under the auspices of Trade Africa, we will establish a more strategic and coordinated approach to trade and investment capacity building in Africa. We will advance ongoing Trade and Investment Framework Agreement (TIFA) negotiations with countries like Nigeria, South

Africa, and Angola, and build on the recently signed TIFA with Economic Community of West African States (ECOWAS).

The Middle East and North Africa

The revolutions and other changes that swept through the Middle East and North Africa (MENA) have provided new opportunities, as well as new challenges, with respect to U.S. trade and investment relations with MENA countries. In 2014, the United States continued to monitor, implement, and enforce existing U.S. FTAs in the region, pursued TIFA consultations with Tunisia and Algeria, and sought new opportunities to cooperate more closely with Egypt. In 2015, we will aim to advance our bilateral trade relationships with MENA countries such as Turkey, where economic ties have grown steadily over the last 15 years. We will also seek to craft and pursue initiatives that can help lay the groundwork for the greater economic integration among MENA countries which will be critical to the future prosperity of the region.

APEC and ASEAN

The Obama Administration is working hard to expand American trade and investment opportunities around the world. Advancing regional economic integration remains a key objective of APEC, whose 21 member economies collectively account for 56 percent of world GDP. Last year, the U.S. played an active leadership role in APEC, working closely with China, the host country, and APEC partner economies to achieve concrete and meaningful trade and investment outcomes that prevent trade barriers, create more transparent and open regulatory cultures, and reduce trade costs by making supply chains more efficient. In 2015, we aim to build upon this work in the areas of regulatory transparency, promoting trade in environmental goods and services, protecting trade secrets, and educating economies on the damaging effects of localization barriers.

In 2015, the United States also will intensify work to enhance regional trade and investment with partners in the Association of Southeast Asian Nations (ASEAN). To complement robust engagement through ASEAN and other regional fora, the United States will work bilaterally with trading partners across Southeast Asia to address trade and investment barriers and enhance mutual economic growth and development. In June of last year, the United States held a first-ever TIFA meeting with Burma, addressing economic reform, labor rights, and implementation of Burma's WTO commitments. In 2015, a priority for the United States will be to work with the government of Burma to achieve further improvements in the protection of worker rights.

Central Asia

We will build upon the work conducted last year under our innovative plurilateral Trade and Investment Framework Agreement with the five countries comprising Central Asia.

Trade and Development

Promoting economic development by creating trade opportunities for some of the world's least-developed countries today can help to reduce corruption and violence. The United States will continue to work with developing countries to lift people out of poverty and foster opportunity through expanded trade and stronger economic growth. Many regions of the developing world hold considerable potential for economic growth. The Obama Administration's efforts to help developing countries to build capacity to harness the power of trade also helps U.S. producers and exporters by enhancing their opportunities to connect with billions of new customers abroad. Thus, by expanding our trade with the developing world we also support jobs and economic growth here at home.

We will continue to work with developing countries to lift people out of poverty and foster economic opportunity through expanded trade and economic growth.

By expanding our trade with the developing world we also support jobs and economic growth here at home.

U.S. trade preference programs provide opportunities for the world's poorest people to climb out of poverty. In support of this goal, the Administration will work with Congress this year to renew authorization of the Generalized System of Preferences (GSP) program. The oldest and most widely used U.S. trade preference program, GSP helps beneficiary developing countries to expand their economies by allowing many goods from these countries to be imported to the United States duty-free. The GSP program also aids American manufacturing by lowering the cost of imported goods used as inputs in U.S. production. In 2015, the Administration will continue to administer our U.S. trade preference programs in a manner that contributes to economic development in beneficiary countries while also addressing relevant statutory eligibility criteria, such as progress on worker rights and enforcement of intellectual property rights.

In 2015, the Administration will also intensify discussions with Congress and our trading partners, as well as U.S. and African stakeholders, on a seamless and timely renewal of AGOA before it expires later this year. This renewal would include third-country fabric provisions for a sufficient period of time to encourage meaningful investment and sourcing. Created in 2000, AGOA has increased and diversified two-way U.S.-sub-Saharan African trade, helping to facilitate a three-fold increase in non-oil exports from AGOA beneficiary countries to the United States. The United States also will continue working with our AGOA partners to ensure that the AGOA program works effectively to benefit both Africa and the United States and that our trade relationships evolve with developments in the region.

The United States will also continue to lead multilateral efforts to assist least developed countries (LDCs) to better integrate into the global trading system. Recognizing the importance of LDCs achieving their development objectives, in 2015 we will advance work at the WTO to monitor existing commitments so that LDC exporters are able to benefit from preferential trade provisions, grow their economies, and thereby increase two-way trade with the United States.

Public Engagement

In 2015, the Obama Administration will continue to consult with Congress and seek input from a wide range of advisors, stakeholders, and the public at large to develop and sustain U.S. trade policies that support American jobs, strengthen the middle class and increase economic growth. This dialogue is critical at every stage of the negotiating process, including implementation and enforcement of trade rules. Throughout these consultation processes, we seek to craft trade policy solutions that are balanced and responsive to a diverse array of American voices.

In the TPP negotiations, for example, the Administration has already held consultations with Congress on more than 1,600 separate occasions and will continue to consult intensively in 2015. We have and will continue to share texts of U.S. proposals with Members of Congress at every stage of the negotiation. Any member of Congress can read the negotiating texts and receive detailed briefings by our negotiators. The committees of jurisdiction are provided advance copies of draft U.S. negotiating proposals before they are tabled to provide input and feedback. As in any international negotiation, we work to maximize transparency, consistent with negotiating the best deal on behalf of the American people.

The Administration also regularly consults 28 advisory committees established by Congress. These include the President's Advisory Committee on Trade Policy Negotiations (ACTPN), Agricultural Policy Advisory Committee (APAC), Intergovernmental Policy Advisory Committee (IGPAC), Labor Advisory Committee for Trade Policy and Trade Negotiations (LAC), Trade Advisory Committee on Africa (TACA), Trade and Environment Policy Advisory Committee (TEPAC), as well as six Agricultural Technical Advisory Committees (ATACs) and 16 Industry Trade Advisory Committees (ITACs). Amongst the advisory committee members are representatives from labor unions, environmental groups, consumer groups, non-governmental organizations, state and local governments, industry and academia. All advisors have an opportunity to review and comment on all draft U.S. proposals before they are shared with other countries, and are encouraged to provide additional input throughout the negotiations.

Further, the Administration has cast a wider net to draw in the views of stakeholders and the public more generally, and to share information with them. These efforts have included solicitation of public comments regarding negotiation objectives through Federal Register notices, stakeholder events at rounds of negotiations, dissemination of trade policy materials such as press releases, factsheets and statements on the recently redesigned United States Trade Representative website, and direct and constant outreach by U.S. trade officials to solicit, obtain, and incorporate public input in the course of their daily work. These efforts will continue and intensify this year. USTR will continue to engage with a wide array of stakeholders including non-governmental organizations, academia, labor unions, environmental organizations, small and medium size businesses, and consumer groups. U.S. stakeholders will collectively help to inform and guide our trade policy decisions. We will strengthen our relationships with states and localities through enhanced engagement with the National Governors Association, the National Conference of State Legislatures, the U.S. Conference of Mayors, and outreach to state and local elected officials.

Conclusion

The Obama Administration's trade policy is firmly anchored in Middle Class Economics. We are seeking to grow our economy, support good-paying jobs, and strengthen the middle class. We are negotiating tough trade agreements with strong enforcement provisions, helping our workers and businesses compete by eliminating barriers to fast-growing markets representing nearly two-thirds of the global economy. But that is not enough. Americans demand more of their government and their trade policy. After all, the United States is not just a business enterprise. We are a nation of values, born of history, tradition, and a shared understanding of what is right.

The Obama Administration's trade policy is firmly anchored in Middle Class Economics.

We are seeking to grow our economy, support good paying jobs, and support the middle class.

The Obama Administration is working to set a new standard, insisting that our values undergird our trade policy today and in the future, promoting strong labor and environmental standards that protect our workers, oceans and forests. In this effort, we have made important strides forward. We have more to do.

We look forward to engaging with Congress and with the American public to ensure that our trade agenda achieves these goals, and strengthens American leadership in the world.

www.ingramcontent.com/pod-product-compliance
Lightning Source LLC
Chambersburg PA
CBHW080620290526
45790CB00007B/2854